Handling Uncertainties

Secrets to being one step ahead

Joshua O. Okpara

DEDICATION

I Dedicate this book to you. Thank you for choosing
to learn the secrets to handling uncertainties.

CONTENTS

Handling Uncertainties

INTRODUCTION

If you're reading this book, then like me, you have possibly been hit with uncertainty— maybe more than once. The uncertainty of life can drain you emotionally, mentally, physically and even financially.

One minute, everything was working and the next, everything changes. One minute the marriage was perfect, the next you're faced with a divorce. One moment you had a job, the next you're unemployed. One moment you see your friend, partner or family member and the next they are deceased.

The fragility of life can be very troubling to the soul. It affects your mind, will and emotions. It ruins happy moments by causing you to think of what could go wrong. It thwarts creativity by limiting risk-taking in the mind of the entrepreneur or business owner. It affects relationships and marriages. Many chose not to marry for fear of divorce. Some even choose not to have kids for fear of losing them. Dreams have been placed on hold by many entrepreneurs for the fear of failure.

Uncertainty creates anxiety and it affects everyone in various ways. I, myself, have been a victim of life's uncertainty and figured out that although it may seem inevitable, the secret to handling uncertainty is hidden in plain sight. We must uncover these truths that I discovered so we can be able to function effectively and maneuver through life handling uncertainty.

In this book, I will give you some weapons to fight uncertainty and show you how you can maximize your purpose. Herein are the secrets to always being one step ahead.

THE BEGINNING OF UNCERTAINTY

I still remember the day like it was yesterday. It was a sunny Friday with low winds. I woke up and followed my weekly routine as a seven-year-old: pray with the family, read my bible, brush my teeth, head over to the kitchen for breakfast, iron my clothes and walk to school, come back from school, do my homework, eat dinner and go to bed. This was my daily routine, and I had expected today would be no different, but I was wrong.

Everything was the same until I came back from school. Typically, my mom— who was my best friend— would cook dinner while we were all away and I would come back home to a hot, cooked meal, but this time things were different. She was not there, and neither was my dad. There was no one at home. Shocked, I walked to my grandma's house who lived a couple of blocks away from us to find out where everyone could've gone, but no one was there either.

At this point, I started to become a little nervous and frustrated, but more so because I was hungry and hated that the routine had been messed up. I stayed outside of my grandma's porch waiting for someone to come home and answer to why the routine was changed. I figured it could be a last-minute shopping decision, or perhaps my dad, who served in our local church, could've been held behind in our Friday service. Maybe my mom is stuck in traffic from buying all my toys and gifts for my eighth birthday, which was approaching in two weeks. I was wrong.

While waiting for my parents, they were in the hospital waiting for the doctor to give a report on my mom who was dying. I had no idea. I was too young to be told that mom was sick. She always looked happy when we spoke. She never complained about our routine. She was always at home making breakfast and dinner for me. How could she be sick, and I had no idea? Why didn't anyone tell me? How long has she been sick, and when will she be home? These were all the questions in my mind as I waited for my dad to come and pick me up to take me to my mom.

About two hours later, my uncle came and took us to the hospital, which was about 12 miles away from our house. I still remember the strong medicinal scent in the hospital. I also remember seeing a coffin outside about 40 feet away from my mother's room. It wasn't hers, neither was it for her, but it felt creepy. I remember the nurses and doctors pacing back and forth, dealing with other patients as we approached my mom's room. Then I walked in and saw her, my best friend, my favorite chef, laying in the bed with different colored wires attached to her. She smiled as I walked in and motioned for me to get closer. With her hands on my cheek, gazing deeply into my eyes, she told me how proud she was of me and all that is destined for me. Little did I know that she was telling me her last words.

Had I known, I would've paid better attention. However, I had only one concern at the time, "Mom, when are you coming home? Have you bought things for my birthday?" Smirking, she handed me her CD player on the bed as an early present and I skipped outside the room to go brag to my father about my new gift. Unbeknownst to me, that would be the last time I would see my mother. It would be the last day I smelled her scent, tasted her cooking or gazed into her beautiful eyes. My mom died that night. Broken, torn apart, and empty are not enough words to explain the gravity of pain I felt in those moments.

I blamed myself for everything. I should've listened more. I should've asked her more questions about who I am. I should've asked her more about how to talk to women or perhaps how I could cope with losing her. I should've stayed in the room longer. I should've savored her meals more. I could've, should've, would've if I had known, but I didn't. For me it was unexpected. Uncertain.

I spent the next ten years of my life searching for a whole version of myself. A part of me had been ripped apart when she left and I was too young at the time to deal with the grief, so it took me years. Years of pain, depression, anger, resentment, guilt, fear and uncertainty came in. I then became uncertain about everything. Will I die the next day too? Will my father die next unexpectedly too? What's the point of me even going to school when anything can happen? Anything did happen. I lost my mom unexpectedly. I had no clue she would pass, and that pain left a scar in my mind that took years to heal.

I had so many questions for God. How could you let this happen? I thought you were in control. I thought you knew the end from the very beginning. I thought you had the whole world in your hands. How then could you allow this tragedy to befall me? While searching for answers, I stumbled upon more questions: How do I be better prepared for tragedies like these?

How can I be better prepared against uncertainty? Are there weapons that I could use to fight uncertainty, and how exactly do I use these weapons? Then I found my answer— the weapon of certainty.

THE WEAPON OF CERTAINTY

Like me, I am sure you have had to deal with circumstances that led to you become uncertain. Perhaps you lost a loved one, a job, a business, or even your drive and passion. Uncertainty kills passion. It can cause you to lose focus and conviction of what is and have you focusing on what could be. This thought process creates unwanted anxiety and causes stress in the mind of an individual. There is, however, one way to combat uncertainty, and that is through the weapon of certainty.

Certainty is defined as a "firm conviction that something is the case." It deals with information. It is you having the knowledge without a doubt that something is true. Certainty trumps uncertainty and kills anxiety. When you have a firm conviction about something, nothing changes your mind. Many have lost their conviction due to the fragility of life. They have

8

now become unsure of everything. Why? Because they are not aware of the weapon of certainty or how to use it.

Certainty is a weapon, one that must be used to combat uncertainty and the anxiety that comes with it. If your favorite football team was playing in the super bowl against their rivals, and you were there watching the game in real time, you could imagine the anxiety in your mind and the anticipation of expecting victory. Each play will have your blood pumping, each turnover will have you nervous and, if the game is a close one, it'll have you at the edge of your seat anticipating victory and fearing defeat. But what if you already knew the outcome? Perhaps you could time-travel and you already saw that your favorite team was victorious. It would change how you watched the game. It will create a confidence in your mind that causes your muscles to be relaxed. You would probably bet money against your friends and rivals that your team would win. Why? Because you have a firm conviction from what you were able to see in the future that your team won.

That firm conviction then combats every doubt, fear or anxiety in your mind. Now let's be honest, that is not realistic. We do not have the ability to time travel, but the principle still stands. Just like there are uncertain areas in life, there are also areas of certainty. Areas where we can generate a firm conviction that combats anxiety. Although we are limited in time-travel, our creator is not. He spoke about Himself in Isaiah 46:9-10 saying, "Remember the former things of old; for I am God, and there is none like me, declaring the end from the beginning and from ancient times things not yet done, saying, my counsel shall stand, and I will accomplish all my purpose." This is God speaking, our creator. He is saying, "I already know the very end of things. I know it so well that I declare it from the very beginning; therefore, because I know the end of things, I know that I will accomplish my purpose."

Purpose. Let's deal with that word for a second and how this word can be the firm conviction we need to fight uncertainty. You see, purpose is defined as the reason why something is created. God created you and me and gave us a purpose. We see this in Genesis 1:26, "Then God said, let us make man in our image and after our likeness. And let them have dominion over the fish of the sea and over birds of the heavens and over the livestock and over all the earth and over every creeping thing that creeps on the earth. So, God created man in His own image, in the image of God He created him; male and female He created them."

God had a purpose in mind, which was to create you and I for the domination of earth. To manage the fish of the sea, the birds of the heavens and the animals over all the earth. This was his purpose. We are a part of it. Not only that, but we are also a part of a plan that has already been set in motion. Remember, "He knows the end from the beginning, and He intends to fulfil His purpose." That, in turn, becomes our firm conviction irrespective of what we face in life.

It is like the football analogy, only this time, we are the players playing against life, which seems to be our opposition. God— who is the coach of our team, knows the end from the beginning and is not limited to time as we are— already saw the end. He has a firm conviction that we won the game. We, on the other hand, must learn to trust that our end has already been predestined, regardless of what the game looks like, or even if it looks like life is winning. The score has already been predestined. The truth is, although our coach, God, is not limited by time, we are and sometimes the pain of not knowing can be too hard to bear, especially when it looks like life is winning.

THE PAIN OF NOT KNOWING

It seems fairly easy to say, "Well, just trust God. He has your life in His hands," when things are going great, and it looks like you're winning. But, when life is throwing all types of curve balls at you, what do you do? There is a pain that stems from not knowing the outcome of things, especially when a bad outcome seems inevitable.

I call it the pain of not knowing. It is like the analogy of the football player. You want to trust your coach, but you feel as if he is delusional. You're getting tackled from left to right, you have multiple turnovers, and your passes are being intercepted; yet your coach holds on to his firm conviction that you will win. How does anyone believe that? How does anyone trust that? How do you ignore the pain of the tackle, the disappointment of the turnovers, or the anger at the interceptions and simply trust a coach who yet seems so sure?

The pain of not knowing is rooted in not trusting. Any football player would tell you that a team that does not trust their coach is bound for failure. They will not trust the plays that was given to them, they will ignore the timeouts called and they will play according to what they feel is right, which ultimately ends up in the failure of the team.

Where there is no trust, there cannot be effective communication. Trust is needed for effective communication. Trust is necessary between the coach and the team where both parties understand that the win is dependent on their cooperation. The coach sees weak areas of the opposition that the players are blind to. Seeing the game from this viewpoint allows the coach to call out plays that will be most effective in beating the opposition and winning the game. If the team chooses to ignore the coach, that team becomes partially blind in the field, which will lead to their demise.

In the same manner, God— who sees all things, knows all things, and understands that the end will yield success— has given us the plays needed to ensure our already predetermined victory.

These plays are instructions, strategies that need to be applied by us to ensure our success and help alleviate the pain of not knowing. Nevertheless, trust is required, and we must be able to trust even if it doesn't make sense.

Proverbs 3:5-7a says, "Trust in the Lord with all your heart, and do not lean on your own understanding. In all your ways acknowledge Him, and He will make straight your path. Be not wise in your own eyes."

What are you trusting? His instructions. The plays He's giving you. The directions that He tells you to go. Even when it doesn't make sense. Why? Because He, unlike you, knows all things and He already know the outcome of everything, including how you overcome. Isaiah 46:9-10 says, "Remember the former things of old, for I am God, and there is no other; I am God, and there is none like me, declaring the end from the beginning and from ancient times things not yet done, saying, my counsel shall stand, and I will accomplish all my purpose." Not only does He know the very end from the beginning, but He also has the strategies to ensure your success, but trust is needed on your end.

What God says is irrelevant to the one who doesn't trust Him. His instruction would not be useful to the person who doesn't trust it. You must decide to listen to His voice because He is always speaking. Like the football coach, He is always calling out plays, giving out effective strategies that keeps you one step ahead and alleviate the pain of not knowing, but your level of trust must increase. The higher your trust, the lower the pain of not knowing. Trusting the voice of God is a weapon that keeps you one step ahead.

THE WEAPON OF CHOICE

I am always baffled when I read the story of the storm Jesus and His disciples encountered in Mark 4 verse 35-41. It showcased multiple scenes that symbolized just how things could be normal one minute and the next, everything changes. It highlights how uncertainty can become a reality for even people who were physically present with Jesus.

It was evening time; the sun was going down and everyone was tired. Jesus had just got done ministering to crowds, so He told His disciples, "Let us go across to the other side." He was referring to the other side of the sea. So, they left the crowds and got on the boat. I could imagine the relief. After dealing with hundreds, possibly thousands of people, teaching and hearing their problems, what better way to relax than to enter a boat and just ride the sea to the other side? It was nighttime. The winds seemed perfect enough for a ride and it would be a great opportunity to nap. So, they entered the boat and set for the journey to the other side, using this as an opportunity to rest since it was just Jesus and

His disciples. Suddenly, everything changed. A fierce storm arose from the mountains, hitting the sea and causing great waves to arise. The storm was so great and the winds so deadly, it began to break the boat, causing water to fill it. Moreover, they were not close to their destination.

Now imagine how that must have felt. One minute, things seem normal and the next a fierce wind arose and now their life is in danger. What seemed certain now becomes uncertain. They are afraid that they may drown, and to make matters worse, Jesus is asleep on a pillow while all this is going on. It's one thing to be dealing with the fierce winds and the breaking of the boat, but how do you handle the disappointment, anger and resentment from seeing a sleeping Jesus. He was the one with the idea to embark on this journey. He is the one who is supposed to be the son of God, the savior of the world. His words were what they trusted to enter the boat and go to the other side, and now here he is sleeping.

How do you deal with a sleeping Jesus when everything seems chaotic? You may not have been in the water with the disciples, but I am sure you know what it feels like for things to seem normal in your life then suddenly everything changes. Abruptly, your life is now in danger, and you are afraid, confused, and stuck in the middle. Everything that you could imagine going wrong is going wrong. There's no one to turn to, and to make matters worse, God is quiet. As a matter of fact, He is asleep. After all these years of serving Him, how could He let this happen to you, or perhaps your kid, or your business? How could He exist and still allow a storm to enter your life and destroy everything you ever worked for? How do you grow from this? Where do you run to? How do you escape when you feel trapped in fierce winds, and everything is breaking apart?

This is how the disciples felt. They were so frustrated, anxious, afraid, and confused. The disciples rushed to Jesus in their pain and exclaimed in verse 38b, "Do you not care that we are dying?" What a powerful question that was recorded in the scriptures for us to see and learn from. Every one of us, irrespective of our socioeconomic status, has dealt with a storm in our life that has led to us asking billion-dollar questions, "Don't you care, God? Don't you care those things are going wrong in my life and everything is in shambles? Don't you care that things seem uncertain right now? Don't you care that I am afraid and confused? Don't you care?"

They woke Jesus up and asked Him this question, and His response shocked me. "He awoke, rebuked the winds and said to the sea, 'Peace! Be still!' Then He said to them, "Why are you so afraid? Have you still no faith?" How do you respond to such a response from Jesus? Why would you ask me why I am afraid when you could clearly see the breaking in the boat? You can clearly see where everything is going wrong, and you dare ask me why I was afraid?

What exactly was Jesus talking about? Their lack of trust in who He is and in His words. Being the Son of God, who also knew all things, He told them earlier before they embarked on the journey, "Let us go across to the other side." He said this knowing the storm would be there. He said this knowing the winds would come; yet He also knew that He was going to the other side.

This knowledge became the firm conviction He needed to be able to sleep through the storm. He knew that the end would be peace regardless. The storms were so bad that the disciples had forgotten the words of Jesus. The fierceness of the winds and the breaking of the boat created room for doubt, which led them to give in to uncertainty and the thought that they might not make it.

The difference between Jesus and His disciples was choice. They both experienced the same storm but made different choices in the storm. Jesus was asleep while they were panicking. Why? Because the conviction was different. Jesus had a firm conviction that He would make it to the other side of the sea, therefore He chose to sleep.

His choice of sleeping was predicated on His firm conviction. That choice to sleep then became a weapon used in fighting uncertainty. He was not worried about the winds because He knew at the end, He wins. Jesus used the weapon of choice, choosing the belief that He will get to the other side as previously spoken rather than believing the noise of the storm. He declared the end from the beginning by saying, "Let us go to the other side." This statement signified that the success of this journey is already predetermined. The knowledge, trust and belief in this became the firm conviction needed to sleep in the middle of a storm. Despite the uncertainties, Jesus chose to live in the certain. He knew that His success was already predetermined. That knowledge surpassed every other knowledge of what was going on around Him.

THE KNOWLEDGE THAT LEDS TO FREEDOM

Do you know that your success is already predetermined by God? Remember, He declares the end from the very beginning. Since your life has a beginning, that means the end has already been predetermined. The knowledge of that, and the choice to believe that knowledge then becomes a weapon in fighting uncertainty. The knowledge of what you know will always triumph the knowledge of what you don't know.

In speaking of the uncertainties, they were facing for preaching the gospel, Apostle Paul in Romans 8:18 writes, "For I consider that the sufferings of this present time are not worth comparing with the Glory that is to be revealed to us." He then spoke of the suffering's humans had been enduring and the uncertainties that can cause us pain. Verse 22 says, "For we know that all creation has been groaning as in the pains of childbirth right up to the present time." The pain is so strenuous at times, he doesn't know "what to pray for as he ought."

Imagine the kind of pain, trauma, and uncertainty you might be dealing with that you could cause you to lose the knowledge of what to pray for. How do you handle these uncertainties? With certainty, Paul says, "And we know that for those who love God, all things work together for good, for those who are called according to His purpose."

How could Paul be so sure that all things work out for you and me? Because it is tied to God's purpose. Don't forget, God said in Isaiah 46:9-10, "Remember the former things of old; for I am God, and there is no other; I am God, and there is none like me, declaring the end from the beginning and from ancient times things not yet done, saying, 'my counsel shall stand, and I will accomplish all my purpose.'"

Paul could be sure that all things work together for those who love God and are called according to His purpose because God knows all things. He sees all and declares the very end from the beginning. Therefore, if He gave you life, there is purpose in you and that purpose has already been predetermined. You simply must trust Him and allow His word to become your firm conviction.

Allow His word to be the certainty you need to combat every uncertainty in your life.

Despite what it looks like, your end has already been predetermined by Him and His purpose must come to pass. Let this knowledge be your firm conviction as you go through the challenges of life and experience the many curve balls, fierce storms or winds that may come your way. Choose to be firmly convicted that your end is already predetermined by God. Kill that uncertainty with certainty.

ABOUT THE AUTHOR

Joshua Okpara is an entrepreneur, best-Selling author, motivational speaker, Pastor, Husband, Father and Artist.

He is a strategy and business coach who specializes in helping clients find their passion and generate income from it.

He is also the founder of the prestigious organization, The Dedicated Men, that focuses on creating a brotherhood of financially literate leaders, entrepreneurs, scholars and professionals, who know their identity in Christ.

He has written seven best-selling books such as *How to Deal with Real Pain in Real Time, 31 Days to A Better You, She's the one, but you're not the one yet, and The Gift of Singleness*; sold nationally and internationally.

Joshua is known for his charisma, leadership, and his passion for Music. He is married to Charmecia Okpara and together they raise their son Josiah King Okpara. He is currently the Founder/Pastor of The Faith Filled Church, located in Lewisville Tx.

LET'S CONNECT

9 781088 010976